Naval History
and
the Citizen

T0346185

Naval History and the Citizen

by

ADMIRAL
SIR HERBERT RICHMOND, K.C.B.

VERE HARMSWORTH PROFESSOR OF IMPERIAL
AND NAVAL HISTORY AND FELLOW OF JESUS
COLLEGE IN THE UNIVERSITY OF CAMBRIDGE

AN INAUGURAL LECTURE
DELIVERED BEFORE THE UNIVERSITY
ON 25 APRIL 1934

CAMBRIDGE
AT THE UNIVERSITY PRESS
1934

CAMBRIDGE
UNIVERSITY PRESS

University Printing House, Cambridge CB2 8BS, United Kingdom

Cambridge University Press is part of the University of Cambridge.

It furthers the University's mission by disseminating knowledge in the pursuit of
education, learning and research at the highest international levels of excellence.

www.cambridge.org
Information on this title: www.cambridge.org/9781316613108

© Cambridge University Press 1934

First published 1934
First paperback edition 2016

A catalogue record for this publication is available from the British Library

ISBN 978-1-316-61310-8 Paperback

Naval History and the Citizen

A LITTLE OVER A QUARTER OF A CENTURY
ago, Professor Pollard remarked that
"Even within the limits of English History
there are certain subjects which pre-emi-
nently demand our attention; and foremost
amongst these, I place Naval History". The
existence of our Empire, he went on to say,
built up as that Empire has been, and rest-
ing as it does, upon sea power, must depend
upon the true interpretation and appreciation of the lessons of Naval History.[1]

For whom is this "true interpretation and
appreciation" necessary? Surely, it is for
those in whose hands the destiny of this
Empire lies. Those hands are the hands of
the citizen. He is the statesman who directs
and controls policy in peace and war, the
Member of Parliament who discusses it, the

[1] A. F. Pollard, *Factors in Modern History*, p. 247
(1907).

5

Press which criticizes and puts forward the editorial opinion, and the man-in-the-street who reads, and hears, and makes his own contribution to the discussions, and, ultimately, is the deciding authority as to what the strength shall be of that sea power upon which the existence of the Empire rests.

I think I shall not exaggerate if I say that the citizens of the Empire have but little real knowledge of the workings of sea power. They may feel instinctively, or because they have been told, that "the sea is all in all" to them, but it is impossible to read either the discussions in Parliament, or the correspondence which takes place in the Press, without seeing how little their beliefs are rooted in the soil of the records of experience. So we see far-reaching proposals frequently put forward, and decisions of the greatest moment made, which either ignore or contradict, even falsify or travesty, the teachings of naval history; and I have no hesitation in saying that we have in recent years been exposed to some grave perils in consequence of this almost universal ignorance, both in and out of Parliament, of this branch of the General History of the country and Empire.

Let me illustrate what I have in my mind by some—a few only—examples. The question of "blockade" is one. We see the assertion made that "the great weapon" which this country has always used in war is blockade; with the inference that the national strategy employed by our statesmen in the wars of the past has always been to reduce, or assist to reduce, our enemies by a blockade of the enemy nation; to create an investment of the country analogous to the siege of a fortress, by which, through the cutting off, by that measure called "blockade", of all external supplies, such pressure has been brought to bear upon our enemies, either singly or in conjunction with our armies, as to induce a need or a desire for peace.

How far is that assertion supported by the evidence of history? On what occasions has this country established, or attempted to establish, a blockade of the enemy nation? In the three hard-fought wars with the Dutch we did not blockade their country. We fought their fleets in the great struggle of 1652–4, and when those fleets were defeated their commerce, deprived of its protection, ceased to sail, and the blow was vital, for the United Provinces depended for their existence upon trade and fishing. But this was not "blockade", nor was a blockade ever declared.

The Tory policy in the wars against Louis XIV was one of using our strength at sea against the enemy's colonies and commerce, thereby depriving France of its sources of revenue; but again, there was no blockade though great efforts were made to prevent food-stuffs reaching the country. When Alberoni, in 1718, attempted to seize Sicily, we did not try to force him to desist from this act by a blockade of Spain. A Spanish fleet, upon which the communications of the Spanish army in Sicily depended, was destroyed at Passaro, and our naval power was then employed to support the troops of our Austrian ally in Sicily in ejecting the invaders. When we quarrelled with Spain in 1739 over a matter of the immunity of our traders, engaged only too often in shady transactions, we did not proceed at once to impose a blockade upon Spain. Our strategical effort consisted in the despatch of an expedition whose object it was to deprive Spain of what Walpole called some "place of consequence"—Havana or Carthagena—thereby to induce her, by the loss of revenue she would suffer from the capture, to accede to our claims for compensation and for "No search". We did indeed send squadrons off Cadiz, Barcelona and Ferrol, but this was with the definite purpose of preventing the Spanish squadrons from falling on our expedition in the Caribbean, attacking our trade, or sending armies either to invade England or capture our naval bases, Gibraltar and Minorca.

When the European war of the Austrian

9

Succession was superposed upon the Anglo-Spanish in 1740–1 we still did not establish a "blockade of Spain". We assisted the armies of Maria Theresa and Charles Emanuel in Italy by preventing the Spanish armies from using the easy and economical route by sea into Italy, obliging them instead to make their way by either the difficult Alpine roads or those along the coast which could be dominated by the guns of the fleet. In the final stage, when France and ourselves became "principals" in the war, we did not try to blockade France. We had indeed to struggle hard for our own security; to guard ourselves against invasion, to protect our trade, to prevent French help reaching the Jacobites in Scotland or Yorkshire during the '45, or French expeditions from injuring and capturing our possessions and settlements in the Northern Colonies and in India. The dispositions of our fleet aimed it at the enemy fleets. The British squadrons were so placed that the enemy squadrons were either confined to harbour by superior force or brought to battle with advantage if they put to sea; and the result of this was that the French commercial flag disappeared from the sea for want of protection from its fighting brother. But neutral traders continued to ply and to carry the goods the enemy required. The Dutchman, the Lubecker, the Dane and the Hamburgher conducted the sea-commerce of the enemy. This is not "blockade". Restriction of enemy's commercial shipping it was, but it neither constituted a siege of the country, nor fulfilled those objects which a blockade fulfils.

When our interests and those of France came into collision in the Ohio Valley in 1755 what did we do? We did not "blockade France". We sent an army across the sea under the protection of the Navy to assist our colonists, and the Navy prevented French armies from reinforcing their armies in Canada; fulfilling thereby that first and most elementary principle of all strategy of concentrating superior force in the spot we regarded as decisive—Canada. Cruising to the westward, our squadrons covered, like a great umbrella, the line of passage across the Atlantic. As before, the result of this was that French shipping could not sail to or from those ports whose approaches were in the occupation of the British squadrons. But elsewhere it sailed. Trade sailed almost freely in the Mediterranean, and as before the neutral carried the enemy trade freely except in such goods as were classed as contraband or under such restrictions as were imposed by the Rule of War of 1756, that measure which was to be extended, with such far reaching results, into the doctrine of continuous voyage as applied by the Northerners in the Civil War of a century later. There is a fund of naval history in that single measure.

When the English in England quarrelled with their fellow subjects in the North American colonies, blockade was not the weapon we employed to enforce our policy. Such interruption of the Colonists' commerce as there was, was in the form of an embargo on the colonial trade—an embargo denounced by Burke as an outrage. Blockade was indeed suggested. Possibly, but possibly only, it might have been effective, but it was not the great weapon that we employed. We endeavoured to subdue the resistance of the colonists by the use of military force on land. When, in the subsequent years of 1778, 1779 and 1780, France, Spain and Holland successively ranged themselves against us, we neither blockaded nor tried to blockade any one of them. We struck at French interests, and protected our own, in the West Indies. We defended ourselves in India against the immortal Suffren. Against Spain, we had to struggle to hold Gibraltar, and eventually struck her a grievous blow not by blockade, but by the capture of Havana. We deprived Dutch shipping of its protection by defeating their fleet in the North Sea, with the familiar result that her commerce ceased to sail, with the natural effect upon a people whose livelihood depended upon the sea. But this, again, was not the "weapon of blockade". We gave support to Frederick of Prussia to enable him to maintain his struggle, which, for us, was purely a diversion, for so long as France chose to make efforts on land, she could not devote resources to the sea sufficient to regain Canada.

The great war with France tells a similar tale. If a generalization may be made by which to express the higher British strategy of the first phase of that long and varied period, it might be that our aim was to keep the armies of the successive coalitions in the field: and that we did this by furnishing them with the money they needed. Such money could only be derived from trade and therefore our trade must not only continue, it must also increase to enable us to give the needed financial help. If it were to increase it must be secure, and security could only come from the destruction of the fleets and squadrons of the enemy and from depriving those fleets of the positions from which they could act effectively. So the tale of those years is largely one of oversea expeditions. Armies go to the West Indies, to the Cape, to the Helder, to Cadiz and Ferrol: and for what purpose? Primarily to establish firmly our security at sea, upon which the fate of Europe, in its ultimate analysis depended: for if we were insecure and could not trade, we could not give our impoverished would-be allies the financial help without which they could not continue their resistance to Napoleon. This was not blockade, nor is it true to say that if, juridically speaking, it was not blockade, the term blockade may nevertheless be used to describe a strategy the effect of which was to deprive France of the external supports and the wealth that she lacked. It neither aimed at, nor did it achieve that isolation from the sea routes which is the essential characteristic of that form of siege which takes its sea-shape in blockade. How remote indeed it was from blockade, in the sense implied, is the assertion that "blockade was the principal British strategical weapon", may be illustrated from a letter from Admiral Duncan, written in 1797 when he was cruising off the Texel keeping his eye upon a squadron of thirty sail of men of war and a similar number of transports: "We see Dutch ships going in and out every day, as if in profound peace, under neutral colours ...our ships tamely looking on at all this requires more philosophy than most of us are masters of". There is very little resemblance to a blockade in this description of the situation.

A change came over the situation after the Peace of Amiens. During that intense phase of the war between 1803 and 1805 when, single-handed, we were fighting for our life against, first France and later Spain, we did not try to obtain a decision by a blockade of France and Spain. Blockades there were, but they were military blockades. There was the remarkable blockade of the French fleet in Brest by Cornwallis. The fleet in Cadiz was blockaded. Nelson lay

16

off Toulon—though he definitely disowned an intention to blockade a fleet which above all he desired to come to sea and be fought. These were purely military measures, totally distinct from blockade in the form of a siege of a nation as a means of exercising pressure upon an enemy people.

The great duel between the land and the sea which began after 1805 was waged for commerce. The French armies closed the ports of the continent to British commerce. The British fleet closed the approaches to those ports by sea. We did indeed then declare blockade. On May 16th 1806, we declared the coast of Europe from Brest to the Elbe to be subject to the restrictions of blockade; but even that partial blockade, which left untouched all the Biscay ports and the Mediterranean, was applied rigorously to a portion only of the northern coast—the strip between the Seine and the Elbe, along which any neutral attempting to enter a port would be condemned if taken. Elsewhere, neutrals could enter or leave provided they had not been laden at, or were destined for, an enemy port. How little this could be called "employing the weapon of blockade" is shown in a sentence of Collingwood's, who, in 1806, was commanding in the Mediterranean: "There are neither French nor Spanish on the seas and our cruisers find nothing but neutrals *who carry on the trade of the enemy*".

The Berlin decree—a measure of boycott, to use a modern term—was Napoleon's reply. English commerce was to be excluded from the continent and England thereby was to be forced to abandon her resistance. The British reply was a paper blockade of the Orders-in-Council. All ports of France from which British trade was excluded were thereby stated to be "*subject to the same restrictions as if they were actually blockaded in the most strict and rigorous manner*". When in 1809 we substituted new Orders-in-Council for those of 1807, we again declared a blockade, of limited extent, including the coasts of France, the north of Italy, Holland and part of Germany: that is, of those territories which lay under the thumb of Napoleon: but this, absolute as it appeared in character, was so riddled with loopholes in the form of licenses that France continued to receive goods from abroad though not enough to give her the prosperity she urgently needed. The object of all of this policy was, as Mahan justly remarks, not the suppression of all trade, which is the object of blockade. It was an act of retaliation, and was so described and justified by Lord Stowell. A retaliatory act is not to be interpreted as an expression of national policy. We speak to-day of defending ourselves against the bombardment of our cities from the air by a threat of counter-bombardment of those who may initiate such a form of warfare. None can say that this may be interpreted to mean that our national strategy is to bombard the cities and the civil populations of our enemies.

I have related this at some length because

it appears to me to be one of the outstanding examples of a popular misinterpretation of British naval history, with consequential proposals for recasting our system of national defence and for rewriting the laws of war. Thus the argument runs: The use to which we have always hitherto put our sea power has been to blockade the enemy. Modern conditions have rendered blockade impossible. Hence we should endeavour to abolish blockade. Or again: Blockade is no longer possible. Blockade was the weapon our sea power employed. Therefore sea power is no longer our strength, and we should substitute for it some other form of power. An acquaintance with the naval history of the past on the part of the citizen would go far to safeguard the country from the results of policies evolved from syllogisms with a false major premise.

Naval history is of no less importance to the citizen in regard to the national policy governing the defence of his trade. I am not referring to such tactical or strategical matters as convoy, patrols and so forth, in which history repeated itself most faithfully during the last war, in spite of completely altered instruments of warfare. I refer to the broad policy of trade defence, the influence of operations against trade, and the broad general principles affecting the nature and quantity of fighting ships which the security of this vital national interest demands.

About a score of years ago there was a strong movement to procure an abolition of all commerce warfare; a movement which was repeated after the late war. History was called on to witness to the merits of this proposal. All operations against trade in war had been, so it was asserted, useless and ineffective, and in the end had proved more injurious to ourselves than to our opponents. The danger to commerce, so the Lord Chancellor asserted in 1913, will neither always prevent wars, nor shorten war, nor bring war to an end.[1] How far are these

[1] Lord Loreburn, *Capture at Sea*, pp. vi and 12 *passim*.

accusations of futility of this form of war supported by history?

Like so many generalizations, they contain partial truths. It is, indeed, a fact that wars have been fought in spite of the known dangers to which the commerce of the belligerents would be exposed. Man is unfortunately so stupid an animal, however, that all his experience of the many miseries of war—death and suffering, distress at the moment and distress in the aftermath—has been impotent to deter him from going to war. Yet, as the qualifying words "almost always" used by the Lord Chancellor imply, there have been exceptions to the generalization that the danger to commerce will not deter a nation from going to war. Are these exceptions so rare, or when wars have in fact been averted by realization of the losses which commerce would suffer at sea, would the injuries and subsequent effects of such wars have been so slight, that we can dismiss the exceptions as negligible, or not worth taking into consideration? Surely we have had wars enough to make us hesitate before abandoning any measures without which we should have had still more. Is not the citizen interested in this matter? And is there any source from which he can acquaint himself on the subject except history?

This country has passed, during the last two hundred years, through many crises in which war has been uncomfortably close, and he would be bold who should say that the danger which commerce would run if war broke out did not on important occasions play a part in the final determination. In 1727 the Emperor Charles VI refused to help or give countenance to Spain when she attacked Gibraltar. Why? Was he in great sympathy with England, or was he anxious to keep Spain within bounds at sea? Sentiment plays a small part in such decisions. That which played a large, if indeed not the principal part, was that the Emperor particularly wished to avoid a naval war which would ruin the Ostend Company, and by interrupting the treasure fleets would cut off the subsidies from Spain at their source.[1] At the same time, the investment of Porto Bello by a British fleet averted a prolonged war between England and Spain, at a very small cost in life. Spain called off her attack on the Rock, and war, which had not become formal, was nipped in its birth. Why? The only dangers which Spain had to fear from England were those of loss of her commerce. Because of the losses she would suffer, she desisted.

But the threat to commerce did not prevent war twelve years later in 1739. It did not, but it nearly did so. The Convention of the Prado had settled the actual dispute, and the naval preparations made by England had convinced Spain of the determination of Ministers to act if she did not fulfil its terms. The danger to commerce did not prove an effective deterrent merely because the intentions of the British Ministry were mistrusted by the Spanish Cabinet; who

[1] Sir Richard Lodge, *Royal Historical Society Transaction*, vol. XXI, p. 19.

were convinced that Britain meant war whatever Spain might do.

It is again hardly open to question that the reason why war was averted in the disputes over the Falkland Islands and Nootka Sound was that Spanish commerce would suffer injury; for this was the only action, other than military occupation of the disputed localities, by means of which Britain could have employed force against Spain in support of her claims.

Passing to the later times of the nineteenth century, feelings ran high in France in 1840 when Mehemet Ali was threatening Turkish integrity in Syria. But that the difference between England and France was settled without war was due, in no inconsiderable degree, to the injury which French commerce would suffer. The French occupation of Mogador in 1844 brought about extremely strained relations between England and France. Lord Malmesbury records that Canning told him, in September of that year, that on some days there was every possibility of war. It was averted. Commonsense undoubtedly played an important part, in that Mogador was not worth a war. But consequences have their influence even in the exercise of that rare quality, commonsense; which, in the long run, is no more than weighing up whether any game is worth the candle. The occupation of Mogador was not worth the candle of the loss of commerce.

In our own time we can remember with thankfulness that some warm differences with France came to nothing, that the political sores which caused them were healed, and that a spirit of friendship eventually replaced one of almost unceasing hostility for some twenty years. The Mekong Valley dispute, Madagascar, and the situation in Egypt in 1898 were all fraught with danger. I would be very far from saying that the sole reason why our great and proud neighbours did not proceed to extremities was fear in general or fear for her commerce in particular; or that her statesmen did not recognize some elements of justice in the British attitude. But I would most certainly suggest that the consequences to commerce if war should break out could hardly be left out of account. When arguments are nicely balanced in the scales, however weighty they may each be, the addition of any weight to one scale throws out the balance. The issue in each case was not worth the losses which a war would bring. Those losses would have been at sea. Could we be justified in assuming that, as a deterrent, as a steadying influence, the effect of the injury which commerce would suffer was negligible? And who, again, to take a wider view, would say that, bad as the condition of the world is to-day it would be better if France and England had ruined each other in 1895 and 1898?

Danger to commerce was an effective deterrent to war when it was desired to enforce upon Turkey the cession of Thessaly to Greece in fulfilment of the Treaty of Berlin. Gladstone then intended to bring pressure upon Turkey through the medium of her commerce, by the seizure of Smyrna and its Custom House: and, at the time of the Armenian massacres, he again prepared to effect the coercion of Turkey by similar seizures at Smyrna, Salonika, and Crete. To put it no higher, the danger of the financial losses which would follow refusal, on those occasions, helped to keep the peace. Whether financial losses are the result of a bale of goods being taken possession of by an individual at the table of a custom house, or by a differently dressed individual in the hold of a ship on her way to the custom house, is immaterial. Danger to commerce was the solvent.

Thus, though it is an undoubted fact that danger to commerce has not always prevented war when tremendous results were at stake, any more than danger to human life and prosperity has done so, naval history will not support the assertion that it has been "almost always" futile as a preventative of war. The bearings of this past experience upon the future are well worth deep consideration when we are thinking of some means of international action which should prevent war in the future.

That dangers to commerce have not shortened war was a second form of the appeal to history to justify the abolition of war against commerce. The American Civil War does not bear out that contention. But for the Federal blockade, the Civil War would have been longer, more costly in men and money, and, as Mahan has remarked, not improbably would have ended differently. So, too, the action against commerce in 1727, already alluded to, shortened that war. But as a general statement it is true that attack upon commerce has not shortened wars, for commerce warfare is very slow in its operation. A continental nation is capable of sustaining a considerable reduction in its trade: even we were able to sustain a reduction of one-third in our imports in the late war. But if commerce warfare has not shortened wars, it has played an appreciable part in the preservation of the liberty of Europe which was at stake in these great wars. Speculation as to might-have-beens may be of little value—a pleasant exercise for the imagination and no more. But it is worth recollecting how high a value was always attached to the attitude of the Maritime Powers in the past. Those were the Powers whose ability to influence the course of affairs lay almost entirely in their power to restrict the movements of commerce by sea; for though Britain could make diversionary and other use of her small army, the United Provinces had no other weapon than their fighting fleet, and no use to which that fleet could be put than the control of sea communications. Prolongation of war is, moreover, not to be regarded wholly on the debit side, for what it has often been in practice is prolongation of resistance to the attempts of a would-be universal conqueror. A continental ruler who should consider making an aggression upon his neighbours wishes above all to gain a rapid victory. He does not wish to pay a great price for his victory. A short, successful campaign is his ideal. A long drawn out, an expensive, war is the reverse. When Louis XV in 1743 was turning his attention to an annexation of the Austrian Netherlands, Marshal de Noailles seriously warned him whither it would lead him. England would be brought into the war, and this would infallibly lead to a long war, a prolonged resistance would be offered to the French forces, during which France would infallibly suffer in her commerce. France was already burdened with debt and internal distress, and of all things a long war was to be avoided. So pleaded de Noailles, but in vain. The King turned a deaf ear to his warnings that an attack on the Low Countries would cause a war with England, and that a war with England would be long and costly to him at sea. He invaded the Netherlands, the war lasted four years, and, at the end, the Netherlands did not pass into French hands, and French commerce had been swept from the sea.

The late war would certainly have been much shorter but for England's intervention. Equally certainly, it would have been longer but for the pressure brought to bear from the sea upon enemy commerce. Naval history, in fact, reminds us not to confine our attention to the prevention and the shortening of war, but to look also to the effect upon the ultimate issue which is produced by the economic and military restrictions of commerce warfare. It must readily be admitted that only one gifted with supernatural powers would have foreseen the course of the late war. Yet there was experience of another war which possessed many similar features—the Napoleonic Wars of 1806 to 1815. How many of our citizens have any conception of the naval history of that period, or of the use made, or the influence of, the Navy, from the time when Napoleon went to Tilsit until he returned from Moscow? What, I would ask, is the kind of picture which the average educated citizen of this country has of the war of those years? How many have any conception of what the sea power of their maritime country tried to do, or did; what effect the command of the sea had upon the whole course of events? He will certainly have heard of the Peninsular war and will know that a British army marched from Portugal to the Pyrenees. He will have a rather vague idea about some dispute between England and the United States, concerning an undue, and unwise, interference with neutral trade which caused a war in 1812. He may have heard of an attack on Copenhagen, though he may also confuse an operation in 1801 with one of a totally different kind in 1807. And certainly too he will have heard of a battle at Waterloo. But will he have any idea of the policy at sea of British Ministers, of its effect, of how, for instance, naval action in the Baltic affecting Sweden, affecting in turn Russia, affected, in the end of the train of circumstance,

5

Spain, and helped to keep her in the field? Should he know so little of the manner in which his statesmen then used the national weapons? Are the experiences of those times wholly inapplicable to the problems on which he has to vote to-day?

But all this, it may be objected, is diplomatic and economic, not naval or imperial history. That, to my mind, is too narrow a view. Naval history is not in a watertight compartment. It is an integral part of general history. Though it is concerned with battles and cruises, expeditions and explorations, those are not the whole of naval history; nor is it in the technical parts of purely naval strategy and tactics that it holds its major lessons for the citizen, its instruction and its guidance. Its great value lies in what it tells us of the use to which naval power has been put, of the effects produced by naval power, of the manner, in its broadest expression, in which that power has brought about the desired results, and the strength that was needed to do so.

34

Education, we know when we scan the Budget, is costly. I would offer the suggestion that ignorance of naval history may be found to be even more costly still. I wonder —and here I permit myself to indulge in speculation—whether, if there had been a more widespread knowledge of naval history, we ever should have had the Declaration of London, which gave Germany the comfortable feeling of assurance that she could pursue her policy without danger from the sea power whose capacity for effective action had been removed by that measure.

A knowledge of naval history is a shield against wasteful expenditure on local defences. The citizen in an isolated or remote spot fears that he will be attacked from the sea; and he calls out for local defences, either in the form of forts, of large land forces, of ships or of flotillas. Some local defences are necessary, but the idea that by their means security can be attained against major forms of injury is highly dangerous to the pocket. It leads to misdirected expenditure in peace and to disturbance of the direction in war. Few things are more common in the history of past wars than pressing applications for the allocating of naval forces to specific localities. It is perfectly natural that men, whether Governors or Assemblies, or merchants, who have a responsibility either for the safety of a colonial possession or of a branch of local trade, or for citizens who look out to sea from a sea coast town, should visualize very clearly the injury to which they would be exposed if an enemy should appear in their neighbourhood. To their eyes, the locality in which they are, or for which they are responsible, is so important that it seems obvious that it must be the target of an enemy attack. Naval history shows it happening in the West Indies, in India, and the sea commanders or the Admiralty being pressed to detach ships from other services to provide for the defence. In the Crimean War there were outcries for ships to be sent to defend the coasts of England and of India, the public not being able to see that there was no danger to either, so long as the Russian fleet was shut up in its ports.

It never is easy to see the world as a whole: few, in Lord Salisbury's words, study large maps. It would be asking too much of human nature to blame men for inability to see, by the light of nature, that their security does not depend upon the presence of a ship cruising off the coast, but upon some force stationed far out of sight, possibly some thousands of miles away. But naval history, like a picture book, explains by illustrations. Lord Howe gave expression to the teachings of experience when he said that the war with France after 1778 could have been won in the Bay of Biscay. The war which is not so far behind us gave us illustrations of the harmful effects of fears against which an intelligent interpretation of history would have been an effective prophylactic.

Descending to a lower plane of war, an

acquaintance with what has gone before is of service to those citizens who become statesmen in their conduct of war. The great power which the ship possesses in her artillery, ever since the cannon became the weapon of the fighting ship, serves as a constant temptation to employ her as a battering instrument. From the stately ship of the line, with her three tiers of artillery, to her less beautiful modern successor, with her thickly armoured gun platforms, the ship of war gives a natural impression of concentrated power and irresistibility. When an enemy fleet, too weak to offer battle but still a latent power for harm, has taken shelter behind the defences of its base, it seems obvious that this mass of power should be used to destroy those fortifications and dislodge or destroy the enemy who lies behind them. For that enemy is not innocuous. From his security he exercises a constant threat. A force considerably greater has to be maintained in readiness to mark him. In military language, it "contains" a larger, often a far larger, force, in exhausting and generally dangerous conditions, withholding them from other important services and supporting thereby the operations against trade.

So we have seen in almost, if not in all, wars, demands and proposals made that the enemy's fortresses should be demolished by the fleet; and sea commanders being often censured because they withstood such proposals. When a Spanish fleet lying in Cadiz was a menace, Nottingham proposed that the fleet should force its way into the Puntales and make an end of it. In 1741 a fleet has been concentrated in Ferrol, and Newcastle wishes the fleet to push into the harbour and destroy it—a proposal countered by citations from naval history which showed the Duke how such operations had been undertaken in past wars. A fleet lying in Barcelona, with an army behind it, threatening Minorca and our allies in Italy, is pointed out as the proper object of attack. In 1855 a fleet in Cronstadt is occupying the attention of a considerable allied fleet, and the Admiral is pressed by Ministers to attack the fortifications: and he comes under a fire of criticism from Ministers and from the Press because he does not lay his wooden walls alongside the stone walls and "crumble the defences to dust".

Sometimes, against his convictions, the seaman gives way. Goaded by criticism or suggestions of personal fear, by reproaches that while soldiers undertake great risks the ships are treated as too valuable to be risked, he undertakes the attack. Ships are sent in against the fortresses at Carthagena, at Havana, at Sebastopol. In each case they have to withdraw, having suffered heavy losses, their spars crippled, their hulls shot through, with many killed and wounded, but with nothing accomplished.

It is noticeable that these proposals occur most frequently in the early days of a war or when an interval of peace has obscured or obliterated the facts and doctrines which were familiar to those who had seen war in progress and heard the experiences of those who had taken part in it. They occur frequently in the early years of the Austrian Succession war. They are rare in the long war with France when those statesmen who had the direction of war had experience to guide them. But they recur in the war of 1854—when forty years of peace had dimmed recollections, or were broken only by bombardments from which it was possible to draw false lessons. Algiers and Acre had been bombarded—why not Sebastopol and Cronstadt? So too, after sixty years of peace, the proposal comes up once more and a fleet is sent to attack the fortifications of the Dardanelles. The old experiences are forgotten or unknown or believed to be inapplicable because some technical developments—some heavier guns, thicker armour, or bombarding contrivances—have come into existence. "If Sir Robert Peel had studied the naval history of the French War", wrote an able sea-officer in commenting upon that Minister's harsh attacks upon Admiral Sir Charles Napier for not having "crumbled the defences of Cronstadt to dust" by fire from his fleet, "he would have learned that Nelson never attacked a battery with ships except very slightly on the first day at Tenerife." If Ministers in 1914 had been better acquainted with the history of war at sea, they might well have thought more profoundly before they sought to force the Dardanelles with ships alone.

To say this is by no means to say that all those things which were impracticable in the past must be regarded as impracticable in the present. This would be to make history a master, instead of a very valuable servant. Naval history tells the citizen certain useful things. It tells him what happened, and why it happened; and while it serves as a corrective to hasty conclusions, it is no less a rich source of inspiration of ideas.

But if it is important, as it seems to me to be, that the citizen should understand and appreciate the use to which the navy of this island has been put by his predecessors, it seems no less important that he should be aware of the relation of the navy to the Empire. The question of whether the hen produced the egg or the egg produced the hen has something of a parallel in our naval and imperial history. Colonies and settlements sometimes begot, and sometimes were begotten by, naval power. Private enterprise took the merchant to India; he was then able to hold his positions there by naval power: and naval power was able to give the protection he needed if it in turn had the necessary footing on shore both in India and on the way thither. Why did we send expeditions to the Cape of Good Hope, to Ceylon and to Mauritius and why do we now occupy those territories? Not for the mere love of expansion or glory, but for the solid and prosaic purpose of ensuring the security of India and the Indian trade. The Cape, in Lord Mornington's eyes in 1800, was simply an outpost to our Indian Empire; in the eyes of seamen it was a position which we could not afford to see in the hands of a hostile sea power. Mauritius, the great French naval arsenal in the Indian Ocean, drew largely its provisions from the Cape, and Mauritius itself was the fortress which sheltered the marauding squadrons which gravely injured the trade of India long after we had established our superiority at sea by the victories in European waters. Ceylon, with its harbour of Trincomali from which a squadron could exercise command of the approaches to India, became a British possession largely for reasons of security at sea. "Whatever may be the riches of Ceylon, the circumstance which renders the possession more particularly valuable for Great Britain is the great facilities which it offers for the preservation of her naval superiority in that part of the world." So wrote a historian of Ceylon in 1815.

Yet, with a wealth of experience to show that the decisions as to who should govern the destinies of India have consistently depended upon the results of the struggles of fleets in the Bay of Biscay and of squadrons in the Bay of Bengal, it is not unusual to find that when "the defence of India" is spoken of to-day, that which is most commonly meant by the phrase is the defence of one frontier only; the land frontier. When I visited the Victoria Memorial in Calcutta, with its picture gallery mirroring the history of India, I saw many pictures of statesmen and judges, administrators, soldiers and merchants on the walls: of seamen there were two portraits, Admiral Watson of the Navy and Commodore Dance of the East India Company's service.

Does this convey to the citizen a true impression of the history of India as a part of the Empire during the three centuries of its association with the British people? If those fierce battles with the enemy and with the monsoons fought by the naval commanders —by Pocock, Steevens, Cornish, Hughes, Rainier and Exmouth—had been lost the fate of India would have been very different indeed.

In every way, in fact, in our history colonies and naval power have been complementary to each other, and the history of the one is a part of the history of the other. Each has its own special branches; the branches of administration and law, of the preservation of order and the developments of local government in the one; the naval administration, the naval strategy and tactics in the other. But in the broad schemes of national policy, of trade, of strategy in its highest application, the two are inextricably bound together. Sea power could not exercise, with any degree of continuity, its influence beyond the limits of the endurance of the ships, unless it had some land-ally who would furnish the shelter it needed, until secure harbours had been acquired for its use: nor could the harbours and the colonies be secure unless the naval strength was adequate to hold the sea roads which separated them from the mother country.

Let me return to what I said at the beginning. We desire to understand the history of the country. If we are rightly to interpret and appreciate the policy, particularly the foreign and colonial policy, of our country, we need to understand the part which the sea has played in shaping the courses we have steered. Naval history is not some separate and specialistic branch, something particular to itself, necessary, perhaps, to the sea officer as military history is necessary to the land officer. It is an integral part of our national history, which we cannot afford to neglect if we are to pretend to a full understanding of the past, or to maintain a wise policy in the future.

www.ingramcontent.com/pod-product-compliance
Ingram Content Group UK Ltd.
Pitfield, Milton Keynes, MK11 3LW, UK
UKHW042141280225
455719UK00001B/8